Diali

Using a spiritualist
the telephone. In :
contact between you and your deceased loved one, as long as you are both there at the right time, willing to communicate, and have a good, clear line of communication and a competent "telephone operator." That operator is the medium, who psychically opens up to receive whatever message is being sent.

Whatever your questions about séances, spirits or the mediums who contact them, this intriguing overview gives you the answers:

- What proof is there of a life after death?
- Can anyone become a medium? What are the first steps to take?
- Is Spiritualism a religion?
- Why are seemingly trivial messages sent to us?
- Why aren't great figures of history contacted more often?
- Can you contact angels through a medium?
- Does your body get "taken over" by a spirit when you're a medium?

The material in this book is based on information obtained over a period of many years from a large number of authentic mediums, and from those who have had "near death" experiences. Find out the *real* truth about spirit communication from those who know!

About the Author
Raymond Buckland came to the United States from England in 1962. He has been actively involved in the study of the occult for more than thirty-five years. He has had twenty books published in the past twenty-three years, has lectured extensively, plus appeared on numerous national and international television talk shows. He is listed in *Contemporary Authors, Who's Who in America,* and many other reference works.

To Write to the Author
If you wish to contact the author or would like more information about this book, please write to the author in care of Llewellyn Worldwide and we will forward your request. Both the author and publisher appreciate hearing from you and learning of your enjoyment of this book and how it has helped you. Llewellyn Worldwide cannot guarantee that every letter written to the author can be answered, but all will be forwarded. Please write to:

Raymond Buckland
c/o Llewellyn Worldwide
P.O. Box 64383-K095, St. Paul, MN 55164-0383, U.S.A.

Please enclose a self-addressed, stamped envelope for reply,
or $1.00 to cover costs.
If outside U.S.A., enclose international postal reply coupon.

Free Catalog from Llewellyn
For more than 90 years Llewellyn has brought its readers knowledge in the fields of metaphysics and human potential. Learn about the newest books in spiritual guidance, natural healing, astrology, occult philosophy, and more. Enjoy book reviews, new age articles, a calendar of events, plus current products and services. To get your free copy of *Llewellyn's New Worlds of Mind and Spirit,* send your name and address to:

Llewellyn's New Worlds of Mind and Spirit
P.O. Box 64383-K095, St. Paul, MN 55164-0383, U.S.A.

LLEWELLYN'S VANGUARD SERIES

The Truth About

SPIRIT COMMUNICATION

by Raymond Buckland

Author of
Doors to Other Worlds

1995
Llewellyn Publications
St. Paul, MN 55164-0383, U.S.A.

The Truth About Spirit Communication. Copyright © 1995 Llewellyn Publications. All rights reserved. Printed in the United States of America. No part of this book may be reproduced or used in any manner whatsoever without written permission from Llewellyn Publications, except in the case of brief quotations embodied in critical articles and reviews.

For permission, or for serialization, condensation, or for adaptations, write the Publisher.

FIRST EDITION
First Printing, 1995

Cover photograph by: Ned Skubic
Quilt design: Vineyard, 1986
    © Rebecca Speakes

International Standard Book Number:
1-56718-095-7

LLEWELLYN PUBLICATIONS
A Division of Llewellyn Worldwide, Ltd.
P.O. Box 64383, St. Paul, MN 55164-0383

Other Books by Raymond Buckland
Doors to Other Worlds
Gypsy Dream Reading
Gypsy Love Magick
Practical Candleburning Rituals
Secrets of Gypsy Fortunetelling
The Committee

Llewellyn Publications is the oldest publisher of New Age Sciences in the Western Hemisphere. This book is one of a series of introductory explorations of each of the many fascinating dimensions of New Age Science—each important to a new understanding of Body and Soul, Mind and Spirit, of Nature and humanity's place in the world, and the vast unexplored regions of Microcosm and Macrocosm.

Please write for a full list of publications.

The Truth About
SPIRIT COMMUNICATION

In the popular mind most, if not all, séances and mediums are fraudulent. But just because something is easy to duplicate in a fraudulent manner, does not mean that the real thing doesn't exist. Certainly there has been a long history of people fooled by con artists pretending to be mediums, and bilking bereaved widows and widowers of large sums of money on the pretext of putting them in contact with their deceased loved ones. Yet there has also been a large number of fraudulent insurance salesmen, television evangelist preachers, investment consultants, bankers, politicians, etc.

There *is* a life after death and it *is* possible to make contact with the "spirit world." It is also possible for many—if not most—people themselves to become the medium through whom that contact is made. This book offers information on how to do so.

THE WORLD OF SPIRIT

The picture of the spirit world I am about to present is based on material obtained, over many years, through a large number of authentic mediums, and through material obtained from those who have experienced the "near death" experience.

—LEVELS 4, 5, ETC.—

——LEVEL 3——

——LEVEL 2——
Immediate Afterlife
[Religious concepts: "Heaven," "Summerland," etc.]

——LEVEL 1——
Physical existence [Earth plane]

If we look upon this physical world in which we live as Level One, then when we die we progress onto Level Two. Almost certainly there are other levels to which we later progress (Levels Three, Four, and more), but we won't concern ourselves with those for the moment.

The other levels are not necessarily *above* us, literally, but since many people do think in those terms that is how I've depicted them here. (In fact I think it is far more likely that they exist right here, in the same space, but in another dimension; another frequency, as it were.)

When we die we pass from this plane, or level, to the next, and there we again come together with those we have known and loved in their previous earthly existences. We are reunited with our parents, grandparents, uncles, aunts, and all the good friends who had died before us. It is a wonderful time of reunion; once again being with those we have missed and, perhaps, believed gone for ever.

We find ourselves in a setting much like the one we left here on earth: there are trees and fields, buildings and books, food and drink, just as we had before. We are able to walk the fields and woods or, if we prefer, the streets of our favorite city. The truth is, however, that we no longer actually need these things. They are there only as "spiritual representations" of their earthly equivalents to make our transition easier. Since we are in the world of spirit we do not actually need a chair to sit on, for example, or a house to live in. Yet we find ourselves with these apparently solid things because it would be too traumatic to suddenly be left without them.

Similarly we find ourselves still with our body, as it was in the physical world. Indeed, this is obviously how we recognize those loved ones who come to greet us and help make the transition easier; because they look as they did when we last saw them.

The first "trick" we learn is that we are able to change things; such as to change our "physical" appearance. If we had trouble losing weight here on Earth, we can become slim simply by wishing it on Level Two. If we were old and bald when we made the transition, we can quickly take on a young and virile appearance from the days of our youth. If we were physically handicapped, we can be whole again. All by simply wishing that it be so. In the physical world, on Level One, we can create our own reality, though it usually takes most of us a while to do so. But on Level Two we can create what we want immediately.

How long we stay on Level Two probably varies from person to person (or "spirit to spirit"). It must also be remembered that there is no such thing as time there; time being simply a human-made convenience. Those who believe in reincarnation feel that this second level is where we review what we have learned in our past life and plan what we need to do in our next life. But whether immediately or after a number of visits back to Level One, we eventually move on to Level Three, and then, probably, on further to other levels.

It seems that we do not come face to face with Divinity, in whatever shape or form He or She manifests, on Level Two. It is almost certainly much further up the chain that we do.

NEED TO COMMUNICATE

On this earthly level, when a loved one dies we mourn and miss them. Too late, we often wish there was some way to tell them how much we loved them. We often resent the fact that they've been taken from us before we've had a chance to share all the things we wanted to share.

On Level Two the deceased have similar reactions. They, too, realize that now they have lost that chance to share their feelings. There is a need and a strong desire to make contact again. It is when that desire is sufficiently strong, from both sides, that spirit contact is most likely to be successful. All that is needed is some means of connecting between the two levels.

A BRIEF HISTORY

One of the first mediums whose séance was described in literature was the one known as "the Woman of Endor." Saul's

Raymond Buckland/7

The Famous Fox Sisters.
(Photo courtesy Prints and Photographs Division,
Library of Congress)

consultation with her as described in the Bible, was typical of a spiritualistic sitting, or *séance*, to make contact with spirits of the dead. There have, in fact, been many mediums down through history, but the ones who made the most impact and really brought about the wide spread of spiritualism were the Fox sisters—Margaretta, Catharine, and Leah.

An outbreak of bangs and rappings on the walls of their house in New York state on Friday, March 31, 1848, was what projected the two younger girls and their mother, Margaret, into the limelight (Leah joined in later). It really wasn't that such rappings were anything new—many of their neighbors admitted to having experienced similar phenomena—but that Cathie started questioning the rapper and *getting intelligent answers!* Neighbors who were called in to witness what was going on likewise asked questions and received satisfactory answers. Even after the girls and their mother had left the house to seek shelter elsewhere for the night, a large group of people continued to communicate with the spirit rapping on the walls.

In the following weeks and months methods of communicating were fine-tuned and, in many demonstrations, the girls went on to show their ability to make contact with spirits. Soon others, emboldened by the Fox sisters, admitted to similar abilities and also gave demonstrations.

Sir Arthur Conan Doyle, in his *The History of Spiritualism*, said: "It was no new gift [the Fox sisters] exhibited, it was only that their courageous action in making it widely known made others come forward and confess that they possessed the same power. This universal gift of mediumistic faculties now for the first time began to be freely developed."

Over the years the sudden interest in communicating with spirits of the dead spread to England, France, and the rest of Europe. Innumerable individuals and investigative committees tried to prove that it was all a fraud. Many would-be mediums were caught, but many more were not; in fact they were shown to be genuine.

Some very accomplished mediums developed at this time; among them were Daniel Dunglas Home, Emma Hardinge Britten, Henry Slade, Eusapia Paladino, and Leonore Piper.

Mrs. Hayden, an American medium, visited England in 1852. Mrs. Robert, another medium, soon followed her there. By the following year the table-tipping craze had crossed the English Channel from France and captivated such notables as Faraday, Braid, and Carpenter.

While other mediums arrived from the United States, England started producing its own mediums. The most notable of these—in fact possibly the most notable of all mediums worldwide—was Daniel Dunglas Home.

Queen Victoria took an interest in spiritualism as, earlier, had Abraham Lincoln on the other side of the Atlantic.

It took a while for English mediums to catch up with Americans but eventually there were some excellent ones to stand alongside D.D. Home. The British National Association of Spiritualists was founded in 1873, and the prestigious Society for Psychical Research in 1882. Three years later, in 1885, the American Society for Psychical Research was created.

In recent years we have seen such fine American and British mediums as Eileen Garrett, Arthur Ford, Jean Cull, George Anderson, and the like. There have been exposés of the unscrupulous (always a good thing), but there has also been confirmation of genuine mediums. No matter how many clouds, it seems that the light will always come through.

MEDIUMS

Using a spiritualist medium can be likened to using the telephone. Let's say you have an uncle who lives in Europe. You wish to speak with him. By picking up the telephone and dialing a number, you can make contact. Sometimes there are problems and you need an operator to make the connection (perhaps he lives in some remote country setting with no automatic dialing or similar); sometimes an operator on this side of the ocean is needed with another overseas operator on the other side. Presuming that your uncle is home at the time you make the call, and that he picks up the receiver to take the call, then you have contact.

In spiritual communication there can similarly be contact between you and your deceased uncle as long as you are both there at the right time, willing to communicate, and have a good, clear line of communication, and a competent "telephone operator." That operator is the medium.

A spiritualist medium is one who, by entering into an altered state of consciousness, is able to plug in and make the connections. He or she frequently has a Control/Guide/Gatekeeper/Guardian (the terms vary) who works as the "overseas operator" to bring the party to the line at the other end.

How does a medium make this connection? Simply by psychically opening up to receive whatever is being sent. In fact, many go into a trance in order to give the contacting spirit more or less free rein on the medium's vocal cords and/or muscles. We'll look more at this in a moment.

TYPES OF MEDIUMS

There are many different types of mediums: clairvoyants, clairaudients, clairsentients, physical mediums, direct voice, and so on, each specializing in one particular way to make contact.

CLAIRVOYANCE: This literally means "clear seeing." In his or her mind's eye, the medium sees the spirit making contact but doesn't necessarily hear anything. He or she then relates what is seen. For example, the medium may say: "I see an elderly man. He must have been about seventy to seventy-five when he passed over. He is tall—about six feet—and has slightly stooped shoulders. He is bald but has a small mustache and wears steel-rimmed spectacles. He wears a cardigan vest and is…" A full description of everything seen is given, enabling the person "on this end," the sitter, to recognize the deceased.

CLAIRAUDIENCE: A clairaudient medium may not actually see anything or anyone but does *hear* what is said to the sitter. For example: "I hear the name Emily. She says she's your grandmother. She's asking how Jane is doing. She says you should not mourn for her; she is very happy where she now is. She is with your grandfather, who I also hear giving his love to you…"

CLAIRSENTIENCE: Clear sensing. The medium may or may not see or hear anything but "senses" it. For example: "I get the impression that your mother's uncle was very generous. I seem to sense that he gave a large sum of money to your mother just before he died but he's now very unhappy about the way she used it…" Clairsentience can include the senses of smell, taste, touch, and the emotions.

PHYSICAL MEDIUMS: These mediums are those who produce actual physical evidence of contact with the spirits. It might be by producing knockings or rappings, by utilizing *ectoplasm* (see following), psychokinesis, levitating objects, or even the actual medium, by producing *apports*, or by *transfiguration*.

> *Ectoplasm*—a whitish substance that exudes from the body of a medium, generally from one of the body orifices. It has been documented in that it has been photographed with infrared film in a darkened séance room. It manifests and is utilized by the spirits to lift objects, such as tables and trumpets, or can form itself into the likeness of a hand or of the face of the spirit causing it to be produced. Fraudulent mediums use cheesecloth and fine muslin to simulate ectoplasm.

> *Apport*—An object that suddenly appears in the séance room, supposedly caused to be there by the

spirits. Apports can be flowers, stones, jewels, even living creatures—virtually anything. They are frequently warm to the touch when they first arrive. It is said that they are dematerialized at their source then rematerialize in the séance room.

Transfiguration—A phenomenon that sometimes occurs when the medium is speaking in "direct voice"—the actual voice of the departed spirit. The medium's face will change to the full physical likeness of the spirit speaking through him or her.

While mental, or non-physical, mediumship can generally be produced in full light, physical mediumship is most often done either in complete darkness or with only a small (usually red) light bulb burning. It is said that the darkness is needed to help produce the phenomena and that light can destroy such things as ectoplasm. Fraudulent mediums, of course, make full use of darkness.

MEDIUMSHIP, CHANNELING, PSYCHISM

A psychic is not necessarily a medium, and neither is a channeler.

A MEDIUM—in the spiritualist sense—is the connecting link between this world and the world of the (recently) dead. He or she serves as the medium (or means) through which the spirits may speak to us on this level. Consequently most of the material produced at a spiritualist séance, or "sitting," is of a personal nature for the sitter(s)—the one(s) seeking contact with the deceased. To an outsider, much of this relevant material may seem trivial in the extreme (yet it can be earth-shaking to the recipient). But then the existence of spiritualism is to provide the sitter with the comfort and knowledge that there is indeed a continuance of existence after death, and that it is possible to bridge the gap between the two levels.

Some critics of spiritualism delight in pointing at the seeming triviality of messages received, thinking that the minutia is unimportant. Yet a sitter may find that the medium's mention of, for example, Aunt Rowena's fondness for miniature roses—something known only to close family members—is of extreme importance, for it firmly establishes that it is indeed the spirit of Aunt Rowena.

A CHANNELER, on the other hand, allows an entity to speak through him or her. That entity is seldom a recently deceased friend or relative of one of the sitters. It is more often a character claiming to have come from another galaxy, for example, or even to be composed of a whole group of minds from a different location in the universe. What this entity does is preach or lecture to the assembled audience. The "messages" vary in their complexity and can range from advising how to "save the Earth" to suggesting we give up all our possessions (sometimes to a specified person or organization!) and await Armageddon. The advice is worth what you get out of it. Some channels are very positive, giving generally good, sound advice, while others are suspect in the extreme.

A PSYCHIC is one who has psychic powers (in fact we *all* have these "powers" and can be taught to bring them out) and uses them to advise a client/sitter. This can be done through the reading of cards, palms, crystal-gazing, casting of lots, astrology, or a hundred other ways. There is not necessarily any connection with the deceased in the majority of cases of psychic "readings."

A word of caution. Weigh carefully any and all advice given to you by whomever you are dealing with—a medum, channel, or psychic. Long dead Uncle Wilber doesn't necessarily now have the "in" on the stock market, any more than does the entity ZJK from the planet Tharam know what is going to happen to the whole world in the next ten years. Don't follow any advice that seems to you to be contrary to your own well-being or the well-being of others.

SÉANCE

As mentioned, the word séance means "sitting." It can be one-on-one—just you and the medium—or it can be a group sitting, with a number of people seated, usually in a circle, with the medium. If it is a group, they may sit around a table or they may sit in an open circle. Frequently the sitters all hold hands. If around a table, the hands are often placed on the surface of the table so that all are touching. In this way it is hoped to remove any doubts about the possible use of somebody's hand to produce fraudulent results during the séance.

The sitting usually starts with the singing of a song or songs. It can be anything; preferably something upbeat and happy. (The spirit world enjoys humor and knows that well-placed humor can overcome nervousness and fear.) The purpose is an attunement. It is to bring everyone to much the same energy level; a balancing of the "vibes," as it were. For the same reason—settling the vibrations and creating the right atmosphere—many séance rooms feature freshly cut, fragrant flowers or burn unobtrusive incense.

After the singing there may or may not be a brief group meditation, during which the medium will slip into trance. Or the medium may go into trance without that meditation. All mediums enter a state of altered consciousness. Not all go into an obvious trance, yet some do go into a very deep one called somnambulism. This latter is often the case when the medium is going to speak in "direct voice." In other words, he or she is going to surrender the vocal cords to the spirit so that it can speak, in its own voice, to the sitter(s).

Two or more people using a Ouija board or doing automatic writing are actually having a séance, even though there seems to be no medium present (see following examples).

THE SPIRITUALIST RELIGION

Not everyone who practices spiritualism is a Spiritualist (with a capital 'S'). A Spiritualist is a member of the Spiritualist Church—or one of many small churches frequently affiliated to the Universal Spiritualist Association. At these churches the sitting is usually in the form of a religious service. There may or may not be the singing of hymns and the saying of prayers but the main feature is the address/séance of the resident or visiting minister/medium. Usually the church members fill out small sheets of paper with questions to a deceased loved one. The minister will then go through these papers and make contact with the departed and answer the questions. It has always struck me as fortuitous in the extreme that the minister/medium is able to make contact with every single one of the spirits sought by the regular congregation and usually all of those sought by visitors to the church. (There is often a separation of "regulars" from "visitors.") In my book *Doors To Other Worlds*

(Llewellyn, 1993), I look closely at some of the fraudulent ways some churches operate, though I hasten to say that not all churches are fraudulent by any means.

SPIRITUALIST CAMPS

There used to be a large number of so-called "Spiritualist Camps" scattered about the country. Camp Silver Belle in Pennsylvania and Camp Chesterfield in Indiana were two of the better known.

Such a camp was a gathering place for spiritualists—a place where people could go and meet a wide variety of mediums and sit in on séances of all types. There was frequently a summer season, though some operated year-round. They filled a very real need and many families would spend their annual vacations at a spiritualist camp.

Unfortunately there have been a number of scandals. For example, in 1960 Camp Chesterfield was exposed in an article in the *Psychic Observer* (July 1960), which proved that many of the mediums were fraudulent in the extreme. For a variety of reasons—exposé among them—a lot of the camps closed down. But some are still operating with excellent mediums. For instance, at Harmony Grove in San Diego I encountered the English medium Chris Meredith, who is outstanding.

RESPONSIBILITY OF MEDIUMSHIP

Anyone who takes on the burden of mediumship automatically takes with it a responsibility to those he or she tries to help. That responsibility is honesty. It is important for mediums to constantly be reminded that they are not there for self-aggrandizement. They are not there to show how clever/powerful/gifted they are in being able to communicate with the second level. They are there simply to act as a bridge between the sitter and the deceased. No more.

In forming that bridge, the medium must relay what is received—no more and no less. There must be no embellishment; no invention.

A common, and perhaps natural, fault in a medium is to try to interpret what is received, but this can sometimes actually work against the information. For example, a clairvoyant medium might contact the sitter's deceased uncle and see him doing certain things which should establish his identity to the sitter. The medium might say: "I see him taking something from the region of his waist. Now he is moving his fingers as he holds whatever it is. Now he places it back at his waist."

The sitter might be overjoyed and exclaim: "That must be Uncle Charles! He always wore a pocket watch in his vest pocket. He'd take it out, wind it, and put it back. I've seen him do it a hundred times!" Proof conclusive for the sitter.

But if the medium tries to put his own interpretation on what is seen, the scenario might go as follows: "I see him removing something from his stomach . . . did he have cancer? Now he is fiddling with his fingers; he must have been an engineer, I think. Again he's indicating his stomach. I think he had many problems in that area."

Talking boards

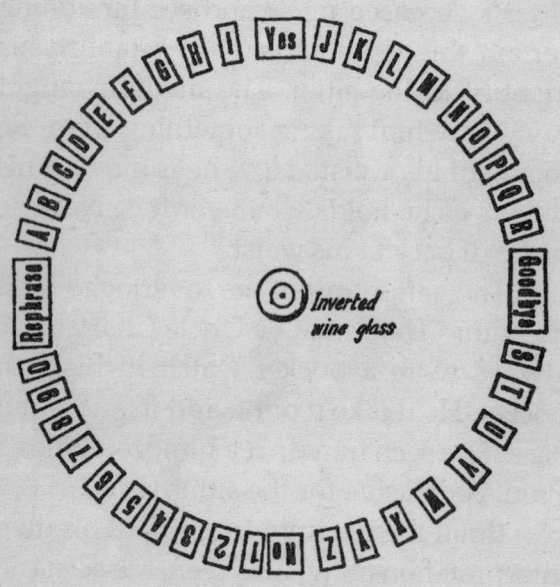

Not surprisingly the sitter is unable to recognize Uncle Charles, who neither had cancer nor was an engineer.

A medium has a responsibility to bring comfort to the bereaved by showing that there *is* a life after death and that we are able to communicate with our loved ones and will, one day, be with them again. This can best be done by presenting what comes through exactly as it is, and not by the medium trying to promote him or herself.

FIRST STEPS TO MEDIUMSHIP

Relaxation is the key to good mediumship and one of the most effective first steps to this is through meditation. There are many different forms of meditation and it really doesn't matter which one is followed.

Start with some general exercises such as head rolls, deep breathing, and progressive body relaxation. With the deep breathing it's a good idea to build a ball of light about you as a protective shield. This is done simply by visualizing white light (or blue, or gold—whatever feels best to you) either coming up from the earth into your body or coming down from "the heavens" into the crown of your head. As you breath in, so the light flows into you, forcing out all negativity. Keep this up until you are filled with the clean, bright light, then keep on for awhile until you are encased in a whole ball of this light. This is a time-tested building of psychic protection. From there go into your meditation, in whatever manner you have been taught.*

TALKING BOARDS

Talking boards, such as the Ouija board, are useful for getting the feel of spirit contact. Much has been written about the "danger" of using a talking board yet it is no more dangerous in the psychic world than is the use of electricity in the mundane world. It should simply be treated

---

*See *Buckland's Complete Book of Witchcraft* or *Doors to Other Worlds*, both by Raymond Buckland (Llewellyn Publications) for detailed methods of meditation.

with caution and not used carelessly. If any spirit coming through the board tries to persuade the sitter to do something that is not in his or her own best interests, the sitter should not do it. It's as simple as that. If such a spirit keeps coming through every time the board is used, the sitter should stop using the board. At least, stop using it for a month or so. By that time the mischievous spirit will have gone elsewhere. If it hasn't, another month should be allowed to pass.

For best results with the Ouija board, four or six people sit around the board, each with a finger on the planchette, or moving platform. The board is placed in the middle of a table.

A simple yet effective "board" can be constructed by simply writing the letters of the alphabet on individual pieces of paper and placing them around the edge of a table.

An upturned wine glass in the center will slide on a wooden table surface and serve well as an indicator.

It is not necessary to be deadly serious when using a talking board. A light, happy approach is best. But at the same time, the planchette should not be manipulated. It's very easy to push it to give answers you want to give, but what is the point? It just wastes everybody's time then. The purpose is to make contact with the spirits and to let them speak. So enjoy what comes, but let it come of its own accord. Don't try to help things.

One person acts as the Spokesperson—all questions being asked through him or her—and another as Secretary, keeping a record of everything asked and everything received.

TABLE TIPPING

A small, light table with three or four legs is best to start experimenting with table tipping. A card table is a good choice. Again, four to six people sit around it, each with their fingers resting lightly on the top edge. As with the talking board, one person acts as Spokesperson. A session starts with asking if any spirit is present. Instructions are given for the spirit to tip up the table onto two of its legs and let it fall back down again, twice for "Yes" and three times for "No." A table can also spell out messages, using one of two methods: (a) by tipping up and falling back on its legs, once for A, twice for B, three times for C, etc., or (b) by the Spokesperson calling out the letters of the alphabet and the table falling as the needed letter is called. Both of these methods are slow and laborious. It's better to ask questions, or have a list of questions prepared beforehand that can be answered simply "Yes" or "No."

AUTOMATIC WRITING

Automatic writing is done by a group or by an individual. With a group, a writing planchette (a small platform on three feet) is needed. Two of the feet are small, rolling or sliding, the other is the tip of a pen or pencil which is sticking through the wood.

The planchette is placed on a very large sheet of paper in the middle of a table (the back of a sheet of wallpaper works well). Everyone then lightly places a finger

Pencil Planchette

on the planchette. With a Spokesperson, questions are asked and the planchette will move so that the pencil actually *writes out* the answers.

For a person working alone, any pen or pencil is held in the hand, in normal fashion. The secret here is for one's attention to be directed toward something entirely different like reading a book, watching television, or talking to a friend. Left to itself, the hand/pencil eventually starts to write. Initially it is just broad scribbling, as the spirit coming through gets the feel of the hand and arm muscles. Gradually, however, words are formed and eventually a message is written out. Later, as the sitter feels that he or she would not be unduly influenced by what is being written, the paper can be looked at as the hand is writing and questions can be asked.

DIRECT VOICE

Direct Voice mediumship is impressive since the sitter hears the actual voice of the departed spirit. Frequently that voice is instantly recognizable to the sitter. Sometimes the voice comes from the medium, the spirit making use of the medium's voice-box, and sometimes it comes from a light tin or aluminum "trumpet" placed in the circle.

Trumpets don't seem to be used as much today as they used to be. They were most often present when the circle was held in darkness and, for that reason, were painted with luminous paint. They could then be seen as they rose up off the floor or table and floated about the circle, coming to a stop near the person to whom the spirit was going to speak. The darkness was necessary, it was said, so that ectoplasm could form and construct an artificial larynx in the trumpet. There are many records of people receiving messages and hearing recognizable voices coming from the trumpet. It was not unknown for a medium to be speaking at the same time that a (different) voice was issuing from a trumpet.

DEVELOPMENT CIRCLES

In the days prior to World War II there were far more mediums than can be found today. Many more people were interested in spiritualism, leading to the development of those mediums. For a wide variety of reasons, interest gradually shifted elsewhere, as spare time became more filled with other things. But indications are that the fascination of spirit communication is slowly coming back.

In the "old days" there were many Home Development Circles. People would

Jack Webber Exuding Ectoplasm.
(Photo courtesy of Psychic Press)

get together with a few friends for the sole purpose of developing their psychic potential and bringing out their mediumistic abilities. They would meet on a regular basis—usually once a week—over a period of years. Such groups are springing up again.

By sitting together with friends in a Development Circle, people can be assured that there is no one present who would act fraudulently or frivolously. All can therefore encourage one another to bring out what talents they have, to experiment with various aspects of spirit communication, to keep records, and chart growth.

RESCUE CIRCLES AND SPIRIT HEALING

Some of the Home Development Circles mentioned above would concentrate their energies on only one or two aspects of psychic development, for example astral projection or healing. Those who developed their astral projection would become what were known as Rescue Circles.

It is known that there are many spirits who, on dying, do not realize what has happened to them for whatever reason; perhaps there has been no one to meet them as they passed over. Consequently the spirit hangs around the area of his or her life. This is the explanation for many hauntings—the ghost is a departed spirit who has not fully departed!

Rescue Circles would make it a practice to go out on the astral and find these "lost souls" and to direct them on along the path. They would usually go out on the astral in pairs and lead many wandering spirits back to the light.

Healing circles are perhaps more common. In fact most spiritualist churches and other groups usually feature a healing session at the end of their regular meetings.

There are many ways of doing psychic healings, but a *spiritual healing* is usually performed by a medium channeling the healing energies of a deceased medico. There have been a number of well—documented cases of seemingly miraculous healings performed by doctors who had left

Level One many years before. Some examples of such mediums are Edgar Cayce, Harry Edwards, and George Chapman.

SPIRIT PHOTOGRAPHY

Departed spirits first appeared in photographs over one hundred and thirty years ago. They have been materializing this way ever since.

The first spirit photograph was taken by William Mumler, who lived in Boston. Setting up a camera to take a photograph of himself, he accidentally tripped the shutter with the camera focused on what he thought was an empty chair. When the picture was developed it showed the transparent figure of a young girl sitting in the chair!

Others began to experiment and soon other spirit photographs started to appear. A very large number of those produced were fraudulent—it was possible to make an appointment with some photographers who guaranteed you would be photographed surrounded by "spirits!"

Polaroid Spirit Photograph.
(Barbara Wolck)

But despite the frauds there were some well-documented photographs and there have been a growing number ever since. Those taken in recent years are invariably strictly controlled so that there is no chance of fraud.

FREQUENTLY ASKED QUESTIONS

What proof is there of a life after death?

There are societies in the United States, England, and around the world which have gathered evidence over many years proving beyond doubt that contact has been made with the spirits of those who have left this earthly life. As one brief example, Harry Houdini spent much of his life exposing fraudulent mediums, yet after his death, he passed back to his wife Beatrice a pre-arranged, coded phrase proving his existence beyond this level. Many other examples are found during the times of great wars, when wives and mothers have received spiritual contact from husbands and sons who have been killed. There are numerous examples such as these.

Can anyone become a medium?

Most people have it within themselves to make contact with departed spirits. Those who work to develop the ability within themselves become adept at it while others may have only occasional flashes of contact.

How long is the training to become a medium?
It varies from person to person. Some people develop a lot faster than others. But we all have it within us to develop this way. When there were many Development Circles held in private homes around the country, the people in those Circles would frequently continue over a period of years. Today we have access to far more books on psychic development than were available fifty years ago. Llewellyn Publications offers many titles that are useful to a would-be medium. Many bookstores, societies, and institutions offer courses in psychic development. Today it need not take a long time to become a proficient medium, though the true medium recognizes the fact that we really never stop learning.

Isn't Spiritualism a religion?

It did not begin as a religion, though later a religion did come into being which was focused on spiritualism. Spiritualist churches are found more often in South America and in England and other parts of Europe than in the United States, although it did not become officially recognized as a religion in England until 1951. Spiritualist churches feature contact with departed spirits and spirit healing as part of their services. Many times the minister is also the medium. But there are also many thousands of people who are interested in spirit communication without formal religious rituals. These latter are also spiritualists.

What Spiritualist organizations are there?

The two largest spiritualist organizations in the world are in Britain. They are the Spiritualist Association of Great Britain and the Spiritualist's National Union. In the United States there is the National Spiritualist Association of Churches.

Is it easy to fake things in darkened séance rooms?

Yes, it certainly is. Which is why many good mediums insist on holding their séances in the daylight, in fully lit rooms or, at the least, in a room with minimum lighting. But just because something can be falsified doesn't mean that in every instance it is fake.

A lot of messages received seem very trivial and don't prove a thing. Why is that?

If the messages you receive personally are trivial and too generalized to mean much to you, disregard them. The medium may not be contacting the spirit he or she thinks (or may not be contacting anyone)! Judge what is received by its content. However, many things received by one person seem trivial to an onlooker yet are especially pertinent to the recipient. As has been stated above, much of the best proof of survival of bodily death is found in the apparent "trivialities" received by sitters.

Why do we get contacted by ordinary people but never by any of the great figures of history?

As has been shown above, we pass from this level (One) to the next level (Two) where we remain an unknown length of time. From Level Two we almost certainly later progress on to Level Three, then Level Four and so on. Presumably these advancements eventually lead to us being at one with Deity. The "great figures of history" have moved on to higher levels, where we can no longer contact them. They have moved on not necessarily because of the "greatness" they achieved here on earth, but simply because of the time (as we judge it) that has passed since their deaths. But recently dead "great ones" have indeed been contacted: Abraham Lincoln, John F. Kennedy, Sir Arthur Conan Doyle, and (dare I say it?) Elvis Presley, for example.

Can you contact "angels" through a medium?

There is no easy answer to this question only because there are many different ideas as to what constitutes an "angel." The ancient Greeks called them *daimons* and regarded them as intermediaries between the gods and humans. They exist in Islamic mythology and were believed in by the ancient Persians. In Hinduism they are referred to as *avatars* and in Buddhism as *bodhisattvas*. The Christian Bible gives contradictory lore, sometimes portraying them as God's messengers, sometimes as bringing God's punishment to humans in the form of sickness and destruction, and sometimes describing angels aiding people. Further, different Christian denominations have diferent concepts of angels. Some spiritualists refer to a medium's "Guide" or "Gatekeeper" as his or her Guardian Angel. Some people refer to their Higher Self as their Guardian Angel.

Does your body get "taken over" by a spirit when you are a medium, like in The Exorcist *movie?*

For the majority of the forms of mediumship—clairvoyance, clairaudience, clairsentience, skrying, healing—the spirit(s) is quite separate and apart from the medium. In such forms as direct voice, automatic writing, talking boards, etc., the spirit may make use of various muscles of the medium, with that medium's permission. Seldom if ever would a medium surrender him or herself totally to a spirit. It is nothing like the movie *The Exorcist*, where the entity invaded the unwilling human's body and had to be driven out again.

What can I read to learn more about spirit communication?

"*Doors to Other Worlds*"—Raymond Buckland (Llewellyn)
> This book contains a comprehensive bibliography on the subject.

"*How to Meet and Work With Spirit Guides*"—Ted Andrews (Llewellyn)

"*Wedge*"—Margaret and Maurine Moon (Llewellyn)

"*Doors of the Mind*"—Michael Bentine (Granada, London)

"*The Life Beyond Death*"—Arthur Ford (Berkley)

"*Many Voices*"—Eileen Garrett (Putnam's)

"The Heyday of Spiritualism"—Slater Brown (Hawthorn)

"The Medium Touch"—Joey Crinita (Donning)

"The History of Spiritualism"—Arthur Conan Doyle (Doran)

On the following pages you will find listed, with their current prices, some of the books now available on related subjects. Your book dealer stocks most of these and will stock new titles in the Llewellyn series as they become available. We urge your patronage.

TO GET A FREE CATALOG

To obtain a catalog, you are invited to write (see address below) for our bi-monthly news magazine/catalog, *Llewellyn's New Worlds of Mind and Spirit*. A sample copy is free, and it will continue coming to you at no cost as long as you are an active mail customer. Or you may subscribe for just $10 in the United States and Canada ($20 overseas, first class mail). Many bookstores also have *New Worlds* available to their customers. Ask for it.

TO ORDER BOOKS AND TAPES

If your book store does not carry the titles described on the following pages, you may order them directly from Llewellyn by sending the full price in U.S. funds, plus postage and handling (see below).

Credit card orders: VISA, MasterCard, American Express are accepted. Call us toll-free within the United States and Canada at 1-800-THE-MOON.

Postage and Handling: Include $4 postage and handling for orders $15 and under; $5 for orders *over* $15. There are no postage and handling charges for orders over $100. Postage and handling rates are subject to change. We ship UPS whenever possible within the continental United States; delivery is guaranteed. Please provide your street address as UPS does not deliver to P.O. boxes. Orders shipped to Alaska, Hawaii, Canada, Mexico and Puerto Rico will be sent via first class mail. Allow 4-6 weeks for delivery. **International orders:** Airmail – add retail price of each book and $5 for each non-book item (audiotapes, etc.); Surface mail – add $1 per item.

Minnesota residents please add 7% sales tax.

Llewellyn Worldwide
P.O. Box 64383-095, St. Paul, MN 55164-0383, U.S.A.

For customer service, call (612) 291-1970.

DOORS TO OTHER WORLDS
A Practical Guide to Communicating with Spirits
by Raymond Buckland

There has been a revival of spiritualism in recent years, with more and more people attempting to communicate with disembodied spirits via talking boards, séances, and all forms of mediumship (e.g., allowing another spirit to make use of your vocal chords, hand muscles, etc., while you remain in control of your body).

Doors to Other Worlds is for *anyone* who wishes to communicate with spirits, as well as for the less adventurous who simply wish to satisfy their curiosity about the subject. Explore the nature of the Spiritual Body, learn how to prepare yourself to become a medium, experience for yourself the trance state, clairvoyance, psychometry, table tipping and levitation, talking boards, automatic writing, spiritual photography, spiritual healing, distant healing, channeling, development circles, and also learn how to avoid spiritual fraud.

0-87542-061-3, 272 pp., 5¼x8, illus., softcvr. $10.00

HOW TO UNCOVER YOUR PAST LIVES
by Ted Andrews

Knowledge of your past lives can be extremely rewarding. It can assist you in opening to new depths within your own psychological makeup. It can provide greater insight into present circumstances with loved ones, career and health. It is also a lot of fun.

Now Ted Andrews shares with you nine different techniques that you can use to access your past lives. Between techniques, Andrews discusses issues such as karma and how it is expressed in your present life; the source of past life information; soul mates and twin souls; proving past lives; the mysteries of birth and death; animals and reincarnation; abortion and pre-mature death; and the role of reincarnation in Christianity.

To explore your past lives, you need only use one or more of the techniques offered. Complete instructions are provided for a safe and easy regression. Make your own self-hypnosis tape, attune to the incoming child during pregnancy, use the tarot and the cabala in past life meditations, keep a past life journal and more.

0-87542-022-2, 240 pp., mass mkt., illus. $3.95

HOW TO MEET & WORK WITH SPIRIT GUIDES
by Ted Andrews

We often experience spirit contact in our lives but fail to recognize it for what it is. Now you can learn to access and attune to beings such as guardian angels, nature spirits and elementals, spirit totems, archangels, gods and goddesses—as well as family and friends after their physical death.

Contact with higher soul energies strengthens the will and enlightens the mind. Through a series of simple exercises, you can safely and gradually increase your awareness of spirits and your ability to identify them. You will learn to develop an intentional and directed contact with any number of spirit beings. Discover meditations to open up your subconscious. Learn which acupressure points effectively stimulate your intuitive faculties. Find out how to form a group for spirit work, use crystal balls, perform automatic writing, attune your aura for spirit contact, use sigils to contact the great archangels and much more! Read *How to Meet and Work with Spirit Guides* and take your first steps through the corridors of life beyond the physical.

0–87542–008–7, 192 pp., mass mkt., illus. $4.99

HOW TO DO AUTOMATIC WRITING
by Edain McCoy

What if someone told you that the answers to nearly all of your most serious questions, deepest fears, and vexing problems could be found locked inside your own mind? And that you could tap into those resources—and all the wisdom of the ages—with little more than a pen, some paper, and a bit of practice?

The divinatory tool you can use to access this knowledge is known as automatic writing: the practice of receiving written messages channeled through your own energy and that of higher intelligences. With the help of *How to Do Automatic Writing*, in less than 60 days you can harness the powers of automatic writing to help better your life, health, finances, and spiritual endeavors.

This book offers a complete course in making automatic writing work for you. Learn who and what you can contact, how to contact them, and how to interpret the messages you receive.

1-56718-662-9, mass mkt., illus., 240 pp. $3.99

HOW TO DEVELOP & USE PSYCHOMETRY
by Ted Andrews

What if a chair could speak? What if you could pick up a pen and tell what kind of day its owner had had? What if you could touch someone and know what kind of person he or she truly was—or sense pain or illness? These examples just scratch the surface of the applications of psychometry: the ability to read the psychic imprints that exist upon objects, people and places.

Everyone is psychic. With a little awareness and practice, you can learn to use your inborn intuitive abilities to read the history of objects and places ... locate missing or lost articles ... develop intimacy... even find missing persons. *How to Develop and Use Psychometry* gives you all of the techniques you need to effectively "touch" the natural psychic within yourself!

1-56718-025-6, mass mkt., 224 pp., illus. $3.99

COMPANY OF PROPHETS
African American Psychics,
Healers & Visionaries
by Joyce Elaine Noll

This is a unique and significant collection of supernatural and ethnic materials never before arranged in one volume! *Company of Prophets* describes African Americans born in the United States who have extrasensory perception, psychic abilities and spiritual gifts, from the 17th century to the present.

This book adds to the historical data not previously available about African Americans, unearthed through recent nationwide interviews and research. It features people from all ages and walks of life, including contemporary and historical leaders in education, business, theology and the arts. They share their experiences with astral projection, soul travel, levitation, healing, past lives, channeling and divination. In their own words, gifted subjects provide practical advice and workable techniques to assist readers in increasing their own psychic awareness.

0-87542-583-6, 272 pp., 6x9, photos, softcvr. $12.95

THE LLEWELLYN PRACTICAL GUIDE TO ASTRAL PROJECTION
The Out-of-Body Experience
by Denning & Phillips

Is there life after death? Are we forever shackled by time and space? The ability to go forth by means of the Astral Body gives the personal assurance of consciousness (and life) beyond the limitations of the physical body. No other answer to these ageless questions is as meaningful as experienced reality.

The reader is led through the essential stages for the inner growth and development that will culminate in fully conscious projection and return. Not only are the requisite practices set forth in step-by-step procedures, augmented with photographs and visualization aids, but the vital reasons for undertaking them are clearly explained. Beyond this, the great benefits from the various practices themselves are demonstrated in renewed physical and emotional health, mental discipline, spiritual attainment, and the development of extra faculties.

0-87542-181-4, 266 pp., 5¼x8, illus., softcvr. $8.95

GHOSTS, HAUNTINGS & POSSESSIONS
The Best of Hans Holzer, Book I
Edited by Raymond Buckland

Now, a collection of the best stories from best-selling author and psychic investigator Hans Holzer—in mass market format! Accounts in *Ghosts, Hauntings & Possessions* include:

- A 37-year-old housewife from Nebraska was tormented by a ghost that drove phantom cars and grabbed her foot while she lay in bed at night. Even after moving to a different state, she could still hear heavy breathing.
- A psychic visited with the spirit of Thomas Jefferson at Monticello. What scandals surrounded his life that the history books don't tell us?
- Here is the exact transcript of what transpired in a seance confrontation with Elvis Presley—almost a year after his death!
- Ordinary people from all over the country had premonitions about the murders of John and Robert Kennedy. Here are their stories.

These stories and many more will intrigue, spook and entertain readers of all ages.

0-87542-367-1, 288 pp., mass market   **$5.99**

THE LLEWELLYN PRACTICAL GUIDE TO THE DEVELOPMENT OF PSYCHIC POWERS
by Denning & Phillips

You may not realize it, but you already have the ability to use ESP, Astral Vision and Clairvoyance, Divination, Dowsing, Prophecy, and Communication with Spirits.

Written by two of the most knowledgeable experts in the world of psychic development, this book is a complete course—teaching you, step-by-step, how to develop these powers that actually have been yours since birth. Using the techniques, you will soon be able to move objects at a distance, see into the future, know the thoughts and feelings of another person, find lost objects and locate water using your no-longer latent talents.

Psychic powers are as much a natural ability as any other talent. You'll learn to play with these new skills, working with groups of friends to accomplish things you never would have believed possible before reading this book.

0-87542-191-1, 272 pp., 5¼x8, illus., softcvr. $8.95